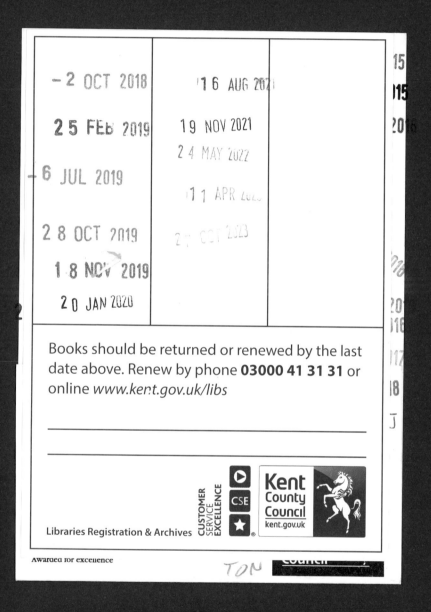

Wild Predators!

Birds of Prey

Andrew Solway

H **www.heinemann.co.uk/library**
Visit our website to find out more information about **Heinemann Library** books.

To order:
☎ Phone 44 (0) 1865 888066
🖹 Send a fax to 44 (0) 1865 314091
💻 Visit the Heinemann Bookshop at www.heinemann.co.uk/library to browse our catalogue and order online.

First published in Great Britain by
Heinemann Library, Halley Court, Jordan Hill,
Oxford OX2 8EJ, part of Harcourt Education.
Heinemann is a registered trademark of Harcourt
Education Ltd.

Editorial: Lucy Thunder and Harriet Milles
Design: David Poole and Paul Myerscough
Illustrations: Geoff Ward
Picture Research: Rebecca Sodergren,
Melissa Allison and Pete Morris
Production: Séverine Ribierre

Originated by Ambassador Litho Ltd
Printed and bound in Hong Kong, China, by
South China Printing Company
The paper used to print this book comes from
sustainable resources.

ISBN 0 431 18992 7
08 07 06 05 04
10 9 8 7 6 5 4 3 2 1

British Library Cataloguing in Publication Data
Solway, Andrew
Birds of Prey. – (Wild predators)
598.9'153
A full catalogue record for this book is available
from the British Library.

Acknowledgements
The Publishers would like to thank the following
for permission to reproduce photographs:
Ardea/S Roberts p33 top; Bruce Coleman/Tom
Brakefield p23 top; CORBIS/W Perry Conway
pp7, 8; Frank Lane Picture Agency/D Maslowski
p42; Frank Lane Picture Agency/Don Smith p33
bottom; Frank Lane Picture Agency/E & D Hosking
p31 bottom; Frank Lane Picture
Agency/Fotonatura/W Klomp p40; Frank Lane
Picture Agency/Frank W Lane p35; Frank Lane
Picture Agency/H D Brandl p41; Frank Lane
Picture Agency/John Hawkins pp7 top, 32; Frank
Lane Picture Agency/John Watkins p19 right;
Frank Lane Picture Agency/Jurgen & Christine
Sohns p22; Frank Lane Picture Agency/Martin
Withers p29; Frank Lane Picture Agency/Philip
Perry p14; Frank Lane Picture Agency/Richard
Brooks p4; Frank Lane Picture Agency/Roger
Wilmhurst p19 top; Frank Lane Picture Agency/S
& D & K Maslowski p21; Frank Lane Picture
Agency/Sunset/J McDonald p9; Frank Lane Picture
Agency/T & P Gardner p17; Frank Lane Picture
Agency/W S Clark pp10, 27; Getty
Images/PhotoDisc pp5 top, 5 bottom, 12, 37 top;
Nature Picture Library/Dave Watts p11;
NHPA/Andy Rouse pp26 ,43; NHPA/Ann & Steve
Toon p15 top; NHPA/Brian Hawkes p36;
NHPA/Dave Watts p13 top; NHPA/David
Middleton p20; NHPA/Hellio & Van Ingen pp25,
37 bottom; NHPA/J & A Scott p28; NHPA/John
Buckingham p31t NHPA/Laurie Campbell p13
bottom, 24; NHPA/Manfred Danegger p34;
NHPA/Nigel J Dennis p15 right; NHPA/Stephen
Dalton pp18, 23 bottom, 30; NHPA/Stephen
Krasemann pp6, 38; SPL/C K Lorenz p39; SPL/Pat
& Tom Leeson p16.

Cover photograph of a golden eagle reproduced
with permission of Frank Lane Picture Agency
(Jurgen and Christine Sohns).Title page
photograph of a snowy owl reproduced with
permission of CORBIS.

The Publishers would like to thank Geoff Dalton,
owner of the Cotswold Falconry Centre, for his
assistance in the preparation of this book.

Every effort has been made to contact copyright
holders of any material reproduced in this book.
Any omissions will be rectified in subsequent
printings if notice is given to the Publishers.

Contents

Any words appearing in the text in bold, **like this**, are explained in the Glossary.

Gripping talons, ripping beaks

Many kinds of birds are **predators**. Blackbirds for instance feed on worms, swallows eat insects, herons and seabirds feed on fish, and storks are partial to mice. But none of these are normally called birds of prey. Different birds of prey hunt in different ways, but all use the same weapons – strong, sharp **talons** and a hooked beak.

Hunters by day or night

Two groups of birds are called birds of prey, or **raptors**. One group is the eagles and their relatives (falcons, hawks and others) – the daytime or **diurnal** raptors. The scientific name for this order (group) is the Falconiformes. The other order is the owls (scientific name Strigiformes). Most owls hunt at night, although some are active during the day.

An eye for detail

Diurnal raptors all have superb eyesight. One reason for this is that their eyes are very large. If our eyes were as big relative to our bodies as those of a common buzzard are, for instance, we would have eyes the size of oranges.

Both owls and diurnal birds of prey, like this buzzard, rely on their strong talons for catching **prey**.

The facial discs of an owl are designed to gather the slightest sounds and focus them on its sensitive ears.

Birds of prey probably cannot see much further than us, but their vision is more acute (they can see more detail) and they are very good at spotting movement. An eagle soaring at 500 metres is a speck in the sky to us, but it can clearly see a rabbit or grouse moving in the grass below.

Good listeners

Owls also have large eyes, but they are designed to pick up as much light as possible when it is 'dark' (even on a dark night there is still some light). Although an owl's eyes are sensitive, it cannot see detail at all well. It makes up for this with its superb hearing. An owl's hearing is so good that scientists have found that it can catch a mouse in total darkness by hearing alone.

Scavengers in the sky

Vultures are diurnal raptors, but they are **scavengers** rather than predators. Vultures are masters of soaring flight. They circle high above the ground looking for **carrion**, and watching each other. If one vulture swoops down because it has seen a meal, others nearby will follow, hoping to muscle in on the feast.

Unlike most birds of prey, turkey vultures have a good sense of smell. They can smell an animal corpse from a distance of several kilometres.

Peregrine falcon

Above the streets of New York, USA, a pigeon flies fast and low. It knows there is danger above. On a ledge high above is a peregrine falcon. It sees the pigeon and launches itself into a heart-stopping dive. As it plummets almost to the level of the traffic, it reaches a speed of 145 kilometres (90 miles) per hour. Levelling out, it catches up with the pigeon and plucks it out of the air.

Grey pilgrims

The peregrine falcon is one of the most widespread of all birds of prey. It lives on every continent except Antarctica. Peregrine falcons are about the same size as crows – 35 to 50 centimetres long, with a wingspan of about 100 centimetres. Males are usually smaller than females. They are handsome grey birds with a striking black 'moustache'.

The word 'peregrine' means pilgrim or traveller, and peregrines certainly live up to their name. Many peregrines **migrate** long distances each summer, and young peregrines may wander hundreds or thousands of kilometres from where they were born.

Catching food

Peregrines almost always hunt birds in flight. Usually they hunt birds the size of pigeons or smaller, but they can catch prey the size of ducks. They dive or 'stoop' from a height to catch their **prey**, plucking them from the air or the ground. Their bodies are **adapted** for fast, strong flight, with a narrow tail and pointed wings.

Peregrines and other falcons have a notch in their beaks, which probably helps them to break the neck of their prey.

A peregrine's nest is little more than a shallow scrape of gravel or soil on a cliff or ledge.

The speed at which a peregrine can stoop has been estimated at between 130 and 320 kilometres per hour (80 to 200 miles per hour). Even in level flight a peregrine can reach 110 kilometres per hour (70 miles per hour). Although the first strike is with the **talons**, the peregrine actually kills its prey with a bite to the neck. This is unusual – most birds of prey kill with their talons.

Mating and breeding

Peregrines usually nest on cliffs, but tall buildings make a good substitute, so these birds are found in many cities. The male performs spectacular aerial displays to attract a female to **mate** with. Female peregrines lay 2 to 4 eggs, which hatch after about a month. The chicks take their first flight after about 6 weeks, and 2 or 3 weeks later they are able to hunt for themselves. Peregrine falcons have been known to live for almost 20 years, but 10 years is more normal.

Gyrfalcons, like this one, are bigger than peregrines, but not so agile in flight. Other close relations are merlins, which are half the size of peregrines.

Kestrel

The cars rush by on the motorway, but the bird takes no notice. It hovers above the grassy bank beside the road, riding the wind. Its body and wings twist and sway, adjusting to changes in the air, but its head stays motionless. The kestrel is hunting on the morning wind.

Kestrels around the world use the hovering method of hunting, although there are slight differences between different species.

A perch in the air

Kestrels are found around the world. The most widespread **species** are the Eurasian, American and Australian kestrels, and there are several species in Africa.

Kestrels are falcons, like the peregrine. They are smaller and lighter in build than the peregrines, and they have a wide tail. Kestrels hunt on open ground. A kestrel's favourite **prey** are voles and mice, but if these are not available it will hunt other small **mammals** or birds. They most often hunt by hovering fairly low over the ground, tail spread and body at a steep angle. If there is a wind they may 'poise' – this is like hovering, but the kestrel doesn't need to beat its wings. Hovering or poising gives the kestrel a 'perch' in the air, from which it can watch the ground below.

Second sight

Like most birds (but unlike humans), kestrels can see **ultraviolet** light, and this is very useful when hunting mice and voles. These animals leave urine trails as they move around, probably so that they can find their way back to their burrows. The urine reflects ultraviolet light strongly, so for a kestrel the trails stand out. The kestrel chooses hovering sites where several trails cross, or a site near the entrance to a burrow.

Catching its prey

If a hovering kestrel sees possible prey, it 'slips' out of the air, gliding down at a steep angle. Because it can see the prey's urine trail, it knows where the mouse or vole will run. When it is just above its prey, the kestrel pauses briefly in mid-air. Then, lifting its wings above its back, it drops with outstretched **talons** on to its victim.

Kestrels hunt by hovering because in open country there are few perches. But if there are trees or posts available, it may hunt from a perch. Unlike most **diurnal** birds of prey, kestrels often hunt in the evening, and even into the night if there is moonlight.

A male American kestrel. American kestrels are smaller than their cousins in Europe and Asia. Male and female kestrels are about the same size, but their colouring is different. This is unusual among birds of prey.

Hobby

It is the rainy season in southern Africa. A thunderstorm has just passed, leaving a slow drizzle. Millions of flying termites are emerging from their nests after the storm. Through these clouds of insects, a group of birds fly in graceful arcs, catching termites in mid-air. Every so often a bird will perch, shake itself dry, and fly off again. The northern hobbies have arrived at their winter quarters.

Long-distance travellers

Hobbies are small, long-winged falcons that hunt insects and small birds in flight. Various kinds of hobby live in Europe, Asia, Africa, Australia and New Zealand.

Northern hobbies nest in Europe and Asia then travel thousands of miles south to winter in southern Africa. When most other birds of prey **migrate**, they soar high into the air on warm currents of air, then glide until they find another warm **thermal**. Hobbies fly, rather than soar or glide, for long periods. When they migrate, they follow the routes of swallows and swifts, which they hunt during the journey.

With its long, curved, pointed wings, a hobby in the air looks like a giant swift.

Acrobatic hunters

Hobbies are superb fliers. They can swerve and 'jink' through the air with incredible agility. For most of the year, hobbies feed mainly on large flying insects, such as dragonflies and termites. But during the **breeding season** they also hunt small birds, in order to catch enough food for their growing chicks. Hobbies can catch birds up to the size of starlings, stooping on them from above like other falcons. They can even catch birds such as swifts, which are themselves very fast and agile.

Raising a family

At the start of the breeding season, male and female hobbies form pairs and choose a nest. Hobbies do not build their own nests, but use old nests of other birds. Each evening, pairs of hobbies perform spectacular aerobatics above their nest site, to advertise the fact that this is their area. Sometimes the males corkscrew down almost to the ground, pulling out of the dive at the last moment.

After **mating** the female lays between 1 and 4 eggs. While the female is **incubating** the eggs the male feeds her, and once the eggs hatch he has to feed both the female and the new chicks.

Australian hobbies catch small birds up to the size of a quail (this one has caught a kingfisher). They also eat large insects and bats.

11

Golden eagle

Above a mountain ridge in Scotland, a golden eagle rises from its nest. The bird climbs until it is a tiny speck in the sky, then plunges downwards in a headlong dive. Just above the ridge it pulls out of the dive and rises once more, then dives a second time. The eagle is telling other golden eagles – 'I'm here: keep your distance!'

Mountain birds

Golden eagles are large and powerful birds about 75 to 100 centimetres long, with a wingspan of over 2 metres. They are found in many parts of the world, most often in mountain **habitats**.

For most of the year, golden eagles live in pairs on a **home range**. Once a male and female **mate** they may stay together for life, which can be 15 years or more.

Golden eagles usually build 2 or more nests, called eyries. Pairs often use one eyrie one year and the other the next. After mating the female usually lays 1 or 2 eggs. The eggs hatch one at a time, and often the first eaglet to hatch will eat its younger brother or sister. After about 9 to 10 weeks the young are ready to fly.

Golden eagles are named for the golden feathers on the head and neck. They have a bony ridge over the eye, which shades their eyes from the sun.

A killing grip

Most eagles are large birds with broad wings for gliding and soaring. Eagles kill using just their **talons**. They have a tremendously powerful grip, strong enough to kill a rabbit or hare on the first strike.

Although they often soar high in the air, patrolling their home range, golden eagles usually hunt by flying low over the ground and diving quickly in for the kill. When it catches large **prey**, an eagle will gorge itself, eating enough food for a week. It is then 'fed up', and will not hunt for several days. The phrase 'being fed up' – meaning being bored – comes from this description of birds of prey that have recently eaten.

Like the golden eagle, the wedge-tailed eagle of Australia pairs for life and reuses the same nest sites again and again. The nest is a pile of sticks up to 3 metres deep, with a shallow cup at the top lined with fresh leaves or moss.

Most large eagles eat at least some **carrion**, but for golden eagles it is quite a small part of their diet.

Cause for concern

In the past, farmers and landowners killed golden eagles because they were thought to prey on young sheep. Today golden eagles are protected, but **conservationists** are concerned because their numbers are falling in some areas. The reasons for this are not known.

13

Bateleur eagle

It is early morning on the **savannah**, and the air is still cool. The eagle with the red beak seems to be balancing in the air rather than flying. It tilts first one way, then the other, its wingtips seeming to finger the air. Then it sees a snake emerging from a burrow. **Talons** outstretched, the bateleur eagle drops on its breakfast.

Flying a tightrope

Bateleur eagles are snake eagles. They are smaller than golden eagles (about 60 centimetres long), but their wingspan can be almost as wide. They are quite common on African savannah.

Bateleurs are masters of soaring flight. They often spend the whole day in the air, clocking up around 320 kilometres (200 miles). Bateleurs have very short tails, which means that they cannot use them for steering. Instead, the bateleur tilts from side to side to steer itself or to correct its flight. This tilting flight gives the bird its name (in French, bateleur means 'tightrope walker').

Soaring and gliding

Many birds of prey are experts at soaring and gliding. When a bird soars or glides, it does not need to flap its wings, and so it saves energy. To soar, a bird finds a patch of warm, rising air called a **thermal**. When a bateleur eagle soars, it spreads its wingtip feathers like fingers. This gives it extra lift. Eagles and vultures can spiral up to great heights in a good thermal. Once they are high enough, they can travel by gliding gently downwards.

Snake hunting

Bateleur eagles hunt snakes in the morning, because at this time **cold-blooded** snakes are sluggish and easier to catch. When it attacks, the bateleur raises a crest of long feathers on its head and spreads its wings, to distract the snake from more vulnerable parts of its body. As well as snakes, bateleurs hunt mice, birds and lizards. They also **scavenge** for **carrion**.

Circus acrobatics

Bateleurs pair for life and nest in the same places every year. Bateleurs perform a very impressive **mating** display. They wheel, dip, dive and males sometimes do 360-degree barrel rolls.

Females usually lay only a single egg which hatches after about 55 days. The young bateleur **fledges** 3 to 4 months after hatching.

A young bateleur eagle raises its crest. Young birds have brown **plumage** and a long tail. Each year they **moult**, and with each moult the tail gets shorter and the plumage changes colour. At about 6 years old a bateleur has its full adult plumage.

Bald eagle

It is October on the Chilkat River in Alaska. In late summer thousands of salmon swam up the river to **spawn** – now they have laid their eggs and are exhausted and dying. The trees all along this shallow stretch of river are full of bald eagles. They watch the river intently, looking for the next free meal of salmon.

Hunters, pirates and scavengers

Bald eagles usually live by water, and their main food is fish. They are large birds, 70 to 80 centimetres long with a wingspan of up to 210 centimetres. They live in most parts of North America, but especially in the north-west (Alaska and British Colombia).

A bald eagle hunts in several different ways. Often it soars above a lake or the sea, then flies down in a shallow glide to snatch a fish from the water with its powerful **talons**.

Although they do hunt for live **prey**, bald eagles are always on the lookout for an easy meal. They will often wait for another bird such as an osprey to catch a fish, then chase after the bird and make it drop its catch. The eagle then swoops down to take the fish. Bald eagles are also **scavengers** and feed on **carrion**.

The yellow legs of the bald eagle stand out even in flight. The legs are not feathered, as feathers might become waterlogged.

Nesting and breeding

Bald eagles usually pair up for life, and often return to the same nesting sites each year. In the spring pairs make spectacular display flights together. During these flights the birds may lock talons and fall through the sky, whirling over and over.

After **mating**, the female lays 1 to 3 eggs. The eggs take about 35 days to hatch. The largest eaglet (young eagle) will sometimes kill any smaller brothers or sisters. After 10 to 13 weeks, the young eagles are **fledged** and take their first flight. They stay in the nest area for several months, learning to hunt by watching their parents and occasionally begging a meal from them. The eagles become adults after about 4 years. They can live to the age of 30, but 15 years is more common.

The bald eagle's closest relations are sea eagles. White-bellied sea eagles hunt fish and sea snakes in South-east Asia and Australia.

The danger of DDT

In the 1950s and 1960s, it was found that a **pesticide** called DDT was causing bald eagles to lay eggs with shells so thin that they broke when the parents **incubated** them. Bald Eagles became very rare and their populations have only recently recovered with the banning of DDT. Other birds of prey, such as the peregrine and osprey, were also affected by DDT.

Sparrowhawk and goshawk

A sparrowhawk pops over a hedge and surprises a flock of sparrows feeding in a field. The flock scatter but the sparrowhawk follows one bird, matching its every twist and turn. The sparrow squeezes through a gap in a fence – somehow, amazingly, the sparrowhawk follows. As the sparrow tires, the hawk overtakes it. Reaching out long legs, the sparrowhawk plunges needle-sharp **talons** into its victim's back.

Accipiters

Sparrowhawks and goshawks belong to a **raptor** group known as accipiters. Accipiters often live in forests and woodlands. Their short, rounded wings and long tails make them fast, agile fliers.

Sparrowhawks are about 30 to 40 centimetres long, with a wingspan of 55 to 70 centimetres. They are common across most of Europe, Asia and North Africa. Goshawks are bigger and heavier, but almost as agile as sparrowhawks. They can grow to 60 centimetres in length, with a wingspan of 165 centimetres. The northern goshawk is less common than the sparrowhawk, but it lives in North America, Europe, Asia, Africa and Australia.

The broad wings and long tail of a sparrowhawk are very different from the pointed wings and narrow tail of a falcon.

A female sparrowhawk with her chicks. The male is smaller than the female, but during the **breeding season** he must feed the female and the chicks as well as himself.

Quick off the mark

Sparrowhawks and goshawks hunt in a very different way from falcons or eagles, relying on surprise and speed in a chase. In woodland, they often hide and wait for **prey** to come close. Then they dash out quickly and silently, making maximum use of cover to get close before the prey becomes aware of them.

Goshawks live in dense woodland, but sparrowhawks also hunt in more open areas. They fly low, flipping over or round obstacles such as hedges, hoping to surprise birds on the other side.

Nearly all of a sparrowhawk's prey are birds caught in flight. Females can kill birds up to the size of a woodpigeon. Being bigger, goshawks take larger birds such as grouse, and **mammals** such as squirrels or young hares.

Eggs and young

Sparrowhawks first **mate** at about 2 years old. The female usually lays 4 to 6 eggs. The eggs hatch after about 40 days, and 25 to 30 days later the young are ready to fly. They remain dependent on their parents for food for another 3 or 4 weeks, while they develop hunting skills. Goshawks are similar, but their young depend on their parents for food for 6 weeks or more after they have **fledged**.

Goshawks and sparrowhawks are close relatives, but to this northern goshawk, sparrowhawks are simply prey.

Red-tailed hawk

In the fork of a tall cactus in Mexico is an untidy nest of sticks. Standing around the edge are three birds. They stretch and flap their wings, swaying as they try to balance. Then one spreads its wings and launches itself into the air. Three red-tailed hawks are ready to leave the nest.

Buteos, not hawks

Red-tailed hawks are medium-sized birds, 40 to 60 centimetres long with a wingspan of 110 to 145 centimetres. They are probably the commonest hawks in North America.

Although they are called hawks, red-tailed hawks are not like sparrowhawks and goshawks. They are more adaptable hunters that can soar like eagles, hover like kestrels or hunt from a perch. They belong to a group of daytime **raptors** known as buteos. In Europe, buteos are known as buzzards. In South America there are several large buteos that are often called eagles.

Defending their territory

Like many eagles, red-tailed hawks often pair for life. Most birds of prey have a **home range** around their nest, but red-tailed hawks and other buteos are very territorial. This means that they have a well-defined area around the nesting site, known as their **territory**, which they defend from other red-tailed hawks.

Red-tailed hawks often hunt from a perch. They are the largest of the buteos found in North America.

On patrol

Males usually patrol the boundaries of the territory, diving on any intruders. Females chase off strangers that come too close to the nest.

After **mating**, the female lays 2 to 5 eggs. She **incubates** them for about 30 days, during which time the male brings food to her on the nest. The young red-tailed hawks **fledge** after 6 to 7 weeks.

The red-tailed hawk often makes a rasping croak while soaring.

Soaring, perching and hovering

Red-tailed hawks are often easy to spot because they spend much of their time either soaring or sitting on a conspicuous (easy to see) perch. Their main **prey** are **rodents** and other small **mammals**, but they sometimes eat birds, lizards and insects, and they also look for **carrion**.

Like most buteos, red-tailed hawks hunt in two basic ways. In autumn and winter they usually hunt from a perch. In spring and summer, when there are plenty of warm **thermals** in the air, they more often hunt by soaring. When a red-tailed hawk spots prey, it launches itself downwards in a gentle glide, then suddenly drops when it gets close.

Harris' hawk

A jackrabbit bursts out of a thick, thorny bush, running for its life. But it has no chance: a Harris' hawk dives from a nearby tree and has the rabbit in its **talons** within seconds. Two more hawks fly down from perches nearby, then a fourth hawk comes out of the thorn bush. All four birds worked together to catch the rabbit.

Sociable hawks

Harris' hawks are medium-sized hawks with long legs and a long tail (length 48 to 78 centimetres; wingspan 100 to 120 centimetres). They are sometimes called bay-winged hawks because of the patches of bay (light brown) feathers under their wings. Harris' hawks are related to red-tailed hawks and other buteos. They live in grassland areas with some bushes and trees, and in dry semi-desert. They range from southern South America north into southern USA.

Unlike most other birds of prey, Harris' hawks are sociable – they like each other's company. Small groups of hawks gather at **roosts** together, and in the autumn large flocks sometimes gather. More importantly, Harris' hawks often hunt together. They will even share the same perch, with one bird 'stacked' on top of another!

Big families

New families begin when two related male Harris' hawks put on spectacular diving displays to impress the females. Often the female will pair with two males rather than just one.

Harris' hawks were first discovered as a species by the great American naturalist John Audubon. The birds are said to be named after Audubon's friend, Colonel Edward Harris.

Once a hawk has made a kill it will often eat the animal on the ground, protecting the food with its wings. This is called 'mantling'.

The two males help to build the nest (usually in a cactus or a thorny bush), **incubate** the eggs and feed the chicks. Sometimes one or more of the young (often the males) stay on until the next **breeding season** and help raise their parents' next group of chicks. Sometimes groups of females nest together. The helpers are often males.

Hunting together

In areas where there is plenty of **prey**, Harris' hawks may hunt alone, but often they hunt in family groups. They hunt in different ways, depending on the prey and the **habitat**. In open country they may hunt on the wing, with one bird driving the prey towards the others. In areas where prey animals can hide in bushes, one hawk goes in after the prey, while the others wait on perches ready to make the kill when the prey comes out.

When hunting alone they catch **rodents** such as mice and ground squirrels. In groups they often catch larger prey such as jackrabbits and all the hunters get a share of the meat.

Harris' hawks are popular with **falconers**, because these intelligent and sociable birds are easy to train.

Hen harrier

A male hen harrier flaps slowly over marshland, carrying a dead vole. Ahead of him a female rises from the reeds, calling loudly. The male flies above the female, and suddenly drops the vole. She flips over in mid-air and neatly catches it, then flies back to her nest to feed it to her chicks.

Grey backs and striped tails

Hen harriers are similar in size to Harris' hawks – 40 to 50 centimetres long with a wingspan of 100 to 120 centimetres. Males are smaller than females, and have different **plumage** – males are mostly grey, while females are brownish with a striped grey and black tail. Males and females look so different that at one time they were thought to be different **species**.

Hen harriers live in northern Europe, Russia and throughout North America. In winter they **migrate** south as far as northern Africa, the Middle East and Central America.

The face of a hen harrier looks very owl-like. This is because it has deep eye sockets (facial discs), which gather sound and improve the hen harrier's hearing.

Marsh and moor

Harriers live on moorlands, marshes and other areas of open country. They hunt by flying low over the ground with a slow, flapping flight, searching the ground carefully for small **mammals** such as mice and voles.

Harriers often hunt in areas with tall grasses or reeds, where it is difficult to see **prey**. Harriers use their very good sense of hearing as well as their sight when hunting. They find prey by sound almost as well as owls. Their large wings and slow flight also make them very quiet in the air. This obviously helps when they are listening for prey.

Hen harriers fly with a trademark slow, flapping flight when hunting.

Many mates

Unusually for birds of prey, harriers often nest on the ground, and they also **roost** on the ground. A male harrier often has a **home range** in which there are several females (up to 5), and he **mates** with all of them.

Having such a large 'harem' keeps a male harrier very busy. The females build the nests, but the male must find good nest sites for all the females and then feed them while they are **incubating** eggs. Once the eggs hatch he also helps to feed the chicks. Late in the summer, when all the chicks are growing, a male hen harrier may have to catch 10 times as much food as usual!

In the autumn, hen harriers may migrate to warmer areas, then return to their **breeding grounds** in spring. During the autumn and winter harriers hunt alone during the day, then gather together in **communal** roosts for the night.

Osprey

In the visitor centre in Abernethy Forest, Scotland, people are crowded around a group of TV monitors. On one of them, a male osprey lands on its nest carrying a large rainbow trout. He calls to a female in a tree nearby, and she flies down. In one **talon** she has the tail of another fish, but she takes the male's latest present and flies back to her perch.

Fish-feeders

Ospreys are large, fish-eating birds of prey, 55 to 70 centimetres long with a wingspan of 140 to 180 centimetres. They live in almost every part of the world, although they do not **breed** in South America or Southern Africa.

An osprey's fish-catching methods are spectacular. The osprey circles or glides about 50 metres above a lake or other stretch of water, and when it sees a fish, it dives down almost vertically. It seems to hit the water head-first, but in fact it brings its legs forward at the last moment. Sometimes the osprey goes in so deep that only its wingtips show above the surface.

Once it has caught its **prey**, the osprey flies to a perch to eat it at leisure. The strong **acids** in an osprey's stomach can digest whole fish.

Ospreys are superb at fishing, but often they are robbed of their catch by larger birds such as fish eagles.

An osprey's foot is covered in tough, spiky skin that gives it a good grip on its slippery prey.

Nesting and young

Many ospreys **migrate** to warmer places for the winter and return to their **breeding grounds** in spring. The males arrive first, and begin nest-building. Ospreys often use the same nest sites year after year.

When the females arrive, males mount impressive flying displays. Once a male has attracted a female he brings her fish regularly and she stays near the nest. After **mating** the female lays 2 to 4 eggs, which she **incubates** for about 35 days. The young ospreys **fledge** after about 55 days, but they do not become fully independent until several weeks later.

Gone, then back again

In the 19th century, British ospreys were almost completely wiped out by hunting, and by 1917 there were no birds breeding in the UK. But in the 1950s the birds began to return, and in 1959, after round-the-clock protection of the nest by bird-lovers, two ospreys successfully raised chicks on Loch Garten in the Abernethy Forest, Scotland. Since then ospreys have returned every year, and they have also begun to nest at other sites in Scotland.

Secretary bird

On the African **savannah**, a secretary bird has spotted a snake. It moves towards the snake in a zigzag walk, its wings open, the crest of long feathers on its head bobbing as it moves. The snake hisses and lifts its head, but is confused as to where to strike. Before it can make up its mind the secretary bird attacks, stamping on the snake's delicate skull with powerful legs.

One of a kind

With its long legs, flamboyant head crest and long tail feathers, the secretary bird cannot be confused with any other bird of prey. In the 19th century, secretaries and clerks used to write with quill pens, which they often kept behind their ears. The black feathers of a secretary bird's crest look like a cluster of these quill pens, hence its name. The secretary bird is also a big bird: up to 120 centimetres tall, with a wingspan of over 2 metres. It lives on the African savannah and spends most of its time on the ground.

Long-legged hunter

Secretary birds hunt over open ground. They often walk 30 kilometres (20 miles) or more each day in search of **prey**. Their main weapons are their strong legs, which they use to stamp on their prey with tremendous force.

Secretary birds are well known for eating snakes, but more often they eat mice, lizards, large insects and birds' eggs.

Venomous prey

Although snakes are by no means their only prey, secretary birds will kill and eat any snakes they come across, including highly venomous (poisonous) puff adders and cobras. Their long legs are covered in thick scaly skin which protects them from a snake's strike, but secretary birds are not **immune** to snake venom.

Nesting and breeding

Like most eagles, secretary birds pair for life and use the same nesting sites year after year. They usually build nests high in acacias (thorn trees). Nests can be very large (up to 2.5 metres wide), because the birds add to them every year.

Although secretary birds usually walk rather than fly, they are actually excellent at soaring flight. During **courtship**, pairs often make soaring, swooping and plunging display flights.

After **mating** the female secretary bird lays 2 or 3 eggs. The male feeds the female while she **incubates** the eggs, which takes about 6 weeks. Both parents feed the chicks, but if there are 3 chicks, the smallest one will often die of starvation because it cannot compete with its brothers or sisters for food. Young secretary birds take about 3 months to **fledge**.

Secretary birds choose their nest site carefully so that it is difficult to see and almost impossible to reach from below. This protects the chicks from ground **predators** such as cats, monitor lizards, and large snakes.

Barn owl

A car drives down a quiet country lane, headlights picking out the white lines down the centre. One of the white lines suddenly flies up from the road, and a pair of white wings flash in the headlights. The driver catches a glimpse of a small body held in the **talons** of a barn owl as it flies away.

Barn owls everywhere

Barn owls are found on all continents of the world, except Antarctica and many large islands. Barn owls are between 35 and 45 centimetres long, with a wingspan of about 90 centimetres. They have heart-shaped faces, long legs and feet with a comb-like middle claw. These and other differences set barn owls and their relatives apart from other owls as a separate **family** (the Tytonidae).

Hunting by ear

A barn owl's eyesight is not particularly good, but it makes up for this with its amazing hearing. Barn owls have large ear openings (hidden by feathers) on the sides of the face. The ear opening on one side is slightly higher than on the other. This helps the owl to pinpoint exactly where a sound is coming from.

Barn owls fly a metre or two above the ground when they are hunting, only rising higher to fly over obstacles.

Barn owls usually **roost** alone, in pairs, or in family groups.

Like all owls, barn owls fly silently. This helps them to hear the movements of **prey**. They hunt by flying low over open country, senses alert. When they hear or see a prey animal, they drop down, extending their long legs to grab their victim.

Barn owls most often hunt small **mammals**, but they also catch other animals such as lizards and birds. They usually hunt at night, but when they have chicks they may also hunt in the daytime.

Rearing young

Barn owls do not build nests, but lay their eggs in the roof of a building, a hollow in a tree, or some other safe place. The eggs take about 30 to 35 days to hatch. The chicks hatch in the order that the eggs were laid, so that by the time the last egg hatches the first chick is several days old. If there is plenty of food available, all the chicks survive. However, when food is scarce the chicks that are born later die, because they cannot compete for food.

The Australian masked owl is a relative of the barn owl.

Threatened relations

Of the 17 different **species** in the barn owl family, 6 are in danger of becoming extinct (dying out). They include the Madagascar red owl, which was only rediscovered recently after not being seen for over 50 years. Another species, the Itombwe owl, is found only in a small mountainous area of Zaire.

Tawny owl

Beneath the trees in the dense pine forest it is dark and silent. Then a long, drawn out 'whooo-oo' comes from one of the trees. A few moments later, another quavering hoot comes from a short distance away. A pair of tawny owls are warning others that this is their nesting site.

Familiar owls

Across much of Europe, Asia and North Africa, tawny owls are the most common and familiar owls. They are medium-sized (35 to 40 centimetres long) brown birds with short, rounded wings. Barred owls are similar birds that live in North America. The two owls are close relatives.

Woodland hunters

Barn owls like open country, but tawny owls prefer woodlands. Their short wings are ideal for woodland flying. Tawny owls have also adapted to living in parkland and even in some cities.

Like most owls, tawnies hunt from a perch. They sit silently on a branch, watching for movement and listening for a rustle or squeak. Like barn owls, they have superb hearing, and can catch **prey** in complete darkness.

A tawny owl reaches out with its talons to grasp a mouse.

Making pellets

Tawny owls prefer to eat mice, rats and voles, but they will catch birds, frogs or insects if other prey is scarce. Like all owls, tawnies eat their prey whole. Their food is partly digested, then goes into a tough 'second stomach' called the gizzard. Here, the meat and other softer parts of the prey are digested. The indigestible bits (bones, fur and feathers) are neatly squashed together into a pellet, which the owl then regurgitates (coughs up).

Tawny owl pellets. Scientists can learn a lot about what an owl has eaten by carefully looking through its pellets.

Eggs and young

Like most owls, tawny owls are not great nest-builders. Females lay their eggs in a hollow tree, or in the old nest of another bird. Tawny owls lay between 2 and 7 eggs. If food is scarce they lay fewer eggs; in good years they lay more. As with barn owls, the young tawny owls hatch one at a time, and those that hatch later are less likely to survive.

The great grey owl is a relative of the tawny owl and is found in northern forests around the world. Its small eyes and huge facial discs show it is a night hunter.

Silent flight

Owls have large wings they can use to glide long distances, only flapping occasionally. The lack of noisy wing flapping keeps their flight quiet. An owl's wing feathers are also important for quiet flight. The feathers are soft with 'frayed' edges. They help to smooth out the turbulence (disturbed air) that is the main cause of noise.

33

Eagle owl

Two crows are flying round a large tree, calling loudly and diving towards a particular spot. The commotion attracts more crows, and also starlings, robins and other small birds. After a minute or two, a large shape detaches itself from the tree and swoops silently away, pursued by several crows. An eagle owl has been chased off its daytime roost.

The biggest owls

Small birds chase away eagle owls because they are dangerous **predators**. They are probably the largest and heaviest of the owls. There are about 12 different kinds of eagle owls, all of them with long ear tufts and feathers on their legs and feet. Probably the biggest is the Eurasian eagle owl. It can grow to 70 centimetres long, with a wingspan of 1.5 metres.

Eurasian eagle owls live in most of Europe, Asia and North Africa. They live in a wide range of different **habitats**, from dense **conifer** forests to mountain areas and deserts.

Talons outstretched, an eagle owl comes in to land on a post. Eagle owls do hunt in forests, but they prefer open spaces. They can take prey in full flight as well as from the ground.

Ready to eat anything

One reason eagle owls survive in a range of habitats is because they are not fussy eaters. They mainly eat **mammals** up to the size of hares, and birds, including other owls. They tear large **prey** into big pieces rather than swallowing it whole. But they also eat snakes, frogs, fish and insects – in fact anything they can catch. The eagle owl hunts from a perch and kills with its **talons**.

Nesting and young

Eagle owls tend to stay in the same area all year. They lay their eggs on cliff ledges, in caves or in old eagle or buzzard nests. The female usually lays 2 to 3 eggs, which she **incubates** for about 35 days. The owlets hatch one at a time, and if food is short only the first ones to hatch will survive. The young owls leave the nest after 5 weeks, but both parents continue to feed them for several months. This gives the young owls a chance to learn hunting skills.

Asian fish owls

Asian fish owls are similar in appearance to eagle owls, except that their feet are covered in rough, spiky and scaly skin like those of an osprey, rather than feathers. The Malaysian fish owl is quite common, but one kind, Blakiston's fish owl (right), is reduced to only a few hundred pairs and is an **endangered species**. Blakiston's fish owls can sometimes be as big as Eurasian eagle owls.

Snowy owl

The white furry back of the Arctic hare is barely visible against the snow, but the snowy owl sees it. Gliding up quickly behind the hare, it drops on to the hare's back, **talons** outstretched. The hare tries to run, but the owl flaps its wings backwards, holding it tight. Eventually the hare collapses, exhausted.

Built for the cold

Snowy owls do not look like eagle owls, but in fact the two are closely related. Snowy owls are nearly as large as eagle owls (50 to 70 centimetres). As their name suggests they are white, with flecks of black. They live in the Arctic during the summer, but in winter they are found across much of Canada, Russia and northern Europe. Its thick, fluffy **plumage** keeps the owl warm in the coldest Arctic weather. Even its feet are well covered with feathers.

Snowy owls stay in the same home range all year round, but they occasionally **migrate** thousands of kilometres south if food supplies in the tundra run short.

Day and night hunters

Although snowy owls often catch Arctic hares, their main **prey** are small **rodents** called lemmings. They also eat a wide range of other prey. Birds up to the size of a grouse, weasels, voles and fish are all on the snowy owl's menu. Like eagle and tawny owls, the snowy owl hunts from a perch. It prefers to hunt at dawn and dusk, but during the Arctic summer there is no night at all, and it has to hunt in daylight.

The white plumage of the snowy owl is excellent **camouflage** when it is nesting, hiding it from predators such as foxes.

Nesting and young

In the **tundra** there are no large trees or large bushes, so snowy owls nest on the ground. Female snowy owls lay 2 to 6 eggs in early spring, while the ground is still covered in snow.

Snowy owls are protective parents, and attack intruders that come anywhere near the nest. Despite their care, **predators** kill many chicks. The young owls leave home after 50 to 60 days.

Dependent on lemmings

In the **breeding season** snowy owls are dependent on lemmings, which live in large numbers in the Arctic. Between hatching and **fledging**, a snowy owl family eats about 1500 lemmings. Numbers of lemmings rise and fall in a regular cycle of about 5 years. Occasionally, the lemming population drops at a time when snowy owl numbers are high. When this happens, thousands of owls fly south of their **home range**, looking for new sources of food. The owls may travel as far south as California or China.

Burrowing owl

The weasel sniffs round the burrow, sensing that it is occupied. Then a long, rattling sound comes out of the hole. The weasel pauses, uncertain, but as the rattling begins again it trots off. Minutes later a female burrowing owl arrives at the burrow entrance. She calls to the chicks below, which were saved from the weasel by their excellent rattlesnake imitations.

Long legs, short tail

Burrowing owls live on open prairies and other grasslands from the southern tip of South America to southern parts of Canada. They are small owls, 20 to 25 centimetres long, with long legs and a short tail.

Burrowing owls hunt mainly on the ground, for beetles, grasshoppers and other insects. They have long legs, which allow them to run after **prey** then grab them in their **talons**. They also catch mice, and occasionally frogs and birds. Burrowing owls can also hunt from a perch, or hover and swoop down on their prey. They prefer to hunt in the evening.

Living underground

As their name suggests, burrowing owls live in burrows. They use them to nest in, but also as places to **roost** and hide from **predators**. Usually, burrowing owls take over the abandoned burrows of prairie dogs, gophers, foxes or other animals.

Burrowing owls often rely on other animals for their burrows. In some places burrowing **mammals**, such as prairie dogs, have been killed as pests, and the reduced numbers of these animals and their burrows has affected burrowing owl populations too.

The long legs of a burrowing owl help it to look over the prairie grasses and spot predators.

Breeding

Burrowing owls often **breed** together in groups. At the start of the **breeding season**, males hover and circle in the air to attract females. Once a male and female have paired up, they prepare a burrow for nesting, clearing it out and lining it with dry material. They may prepare several burrows before choosing one for nesting.

Eggs and young

The female lays 6 to 9 eggs and **incubates** them for about 4 weeks. The male brings her food and guards the burrow entrance. The chicks leave the nest after about 6 weeks, but remain in the area, resting and hiding in other burrows close to the nest. The parents continue to feed the young while they improve their hunting skills.

Small and smaller

Although burrowing owls are small, they are not the smallest **species** of owl. Pygmy owls can be less than 17 centimetres long, and the least pygmy owl, which lives in tropical forests in South and Central America, is a mere 12 centimetres. Elf owls, which live in Mexico and parts of southern USA, are similar in size to least pygmy owls.

Long-eared owl

For several days a photographer has been filming the nest of a long-eared owl from a **hide**. On this day, when he first focuses on the nest he sees an extraordinary sight. The female owl is sitting over her chicks, feathers bristling and wings half-spread over her back, looking twice her normal size and very fierce. She is in her threat display, defending her chicks from a hungry pine marten.

Not ears but feathers

Long-eared owls are medium-sized owls, 35 to 40 centimetres long, with a wingspan of about 100 centimetres. They are slim with long wings and a long tail. Their 'ears' are not actually ears, but special feathers, which can stand up or lie flat. Long-eared owls are found in **temperate** regions throughout the northern hemisphere.

Night patrollers

Even more than other owls, long-eared owls are night hunters. They rarely begin hunting before early evening. Like barn owls, long-eared owls hunt on the wing over open ground. They fly low with their head cocked to one side, listening for **prey**.

When a long-eared owl finds prey it pounces straight away, pinning its victim down with its **talons**, then killing it with a bite to the neck. A long-eared owl's preferred prey is mice and voles, but if these are in short supply it will hunt birds.

Long-eared owls are difficult to spot because by day they hide away in thick conifer woodland.

Hidden away

Although long-eared owls hunt over open ground, they like to spend the day well hidden in thick woodland. They especially like **conifer** woods. If they sense danger they stand very straight, with their large ear tufts standing up, so that they look rather like a broken branch on the tree.

Long-eared owls usually nest in thick woodland too. Often they will use the old nest of another bird, such as a crow or magpie. The female lays between 3 to 8 eggs, which take about 4 weeks to hatch. The young chicks usually move from the nest on to nearby branches when they are about 3 weeks old, but they cannot fly until they are about 5 weeks old.

Protecting the chicks

While the chicks are young, the adults will go to great lengths to protect them from **predators**. They make themselves look much bigger in an impressive threat display, which is often effective against possible predators. Older chicks also take up the threat pose if they are disturbed.

If this display does not work, the female owl may try to distract the predator. She pretends to be injured, falling from the tree, crawling along the ground with one wing trailing, and making distress calls.

Young long-eared owls use this impressive display when danger threatens.

Northern hawk owl

A bird flies fast and straight from one perch to another. Its tapered wings look like those of a peregrine. Then the bird rises in to the sky and hovers briefly, like a kestrel. But as it returns to its perch it makes a whistle-like call – "Ulululululululu...". It is not a falcon at all, but a northern hawk owl.

Chubby falcons

Northern hawk owls are medium-sized owls found in open forests and moorlands in northern America, Europe and Asia. They are about 35 to 40 centimetres long.

With its pointed wings and long tail a hawk owl looks more like a chubby falcon than an owl. Its head and face are also quite hawk-like, because it does not have large facial discs around its eyes as most owls do. A hawk owl does not rely on amazing hearing as much as other owls. In fact it often hunts during the daytime, although in the long Arctic winters it must hunt in darkness.

Hawk owls do not have the large facial discs of other owls. This suggests that their hearing is not as good as that of other owls.

The flight of hawk owls is fast and direct like a falcon, not gentle and gliding like an owl.

High perch hunters

A northern hawk owl's main **prey** are voles and lemmings, although they also catch birds. Like the snowy owl, hawk owls may fly south to find other foods when voles and lemmings are scarce. Hawk owls mainly hunt from a high perch, swooping down when they see prey. They may also fly slowly over an area, hovering when they see a prey animal and then dropping down to catch it.

Nesting and young

Northern hawk owls make nests in the hollow top of an old tree stump or an old woodpecker's nest. The female usually lays 5 or 6 eggs and **incubates** them for 25 to 30 days. As with other owls, the eggs are laid one at a time. Once they hatch, the chicks grow quickly – they are ready to fly within a month. The parents continue to feed the chicks for several months after they **fledge**.

Southern hawk owls

In the southern hemisphere there are several other owls that look like daytime **raptors** and are known as hawk owls. Most are medium-sized, like the northern hawk owl (although they are not closely related). But in Australia, where there are fewer other owls, there are several kinds of hawk owl, some almost as large as eagle owls.

Classification chart

Scientists classify the millions of different living things by comparing many different characteristics, ranging from their outward appearance to the chemicals that make up their bodies. They use similarities and differences between living things to sort them into groups.

A **species** is a group of animals or plants that are all similar and can **breed** together. Different species that are closely related are put together in a larger group called a genus (plural genera). Similar genera are grouped into **families**, and similar families are grouped together in orders. Closely related orders are grouped into classes, classes are grouped into phyla and phyla are put together in huge groups called kingdoms. Plants and animals are the two best known kingdoms.

All birds belong to the class Aves. Daytime birds of prey form the order Falconiformes, while owls belong to the order Strigiformes.

Order Falconiformes

Family	Number of Genera	Number of Species	Examples
New World vultures (Cathartidae)	5	7	Andean condor (largest of all raptors), black vulture, turkey vulture, California condor, king vulture
Eagles, hawks, buzzards, kites and Old World vultures (Accipitridae)	65	224	golden eagle, bateleur eagle, bald eagle, sparrowhawk, goshawk, red-tailed hawk, Harris' hawk, hen harrier, osprey
Secretary birds (Sagittaridae)	1 (Sagittarius)		secretary bird
Falcons and caracaras (Falconidae)	7	60	peregrine falcon, gyrfalcon, merlin, hobby, kestrels

Order Strigiformes

Family	Number of Genera	Number of Species	Examples
Barn, grass and bay owls (Tytonidae)	2 (Tyto, Pholidus)	17	barn owl, eastern grass owl, bay owl
Typical owls (Strigidae)	23 (e.g. Strix, Bubo, Ketupa, Nyctea, Speotyto, Ninox, Asio)	about 130	tawny owl, barred owl, eagle owls, fish owls, snowy owl, burrowing owl, hawk owls, long-eared owl

Where birds of prey live

These maps show where some of the birds of prey of the world live.

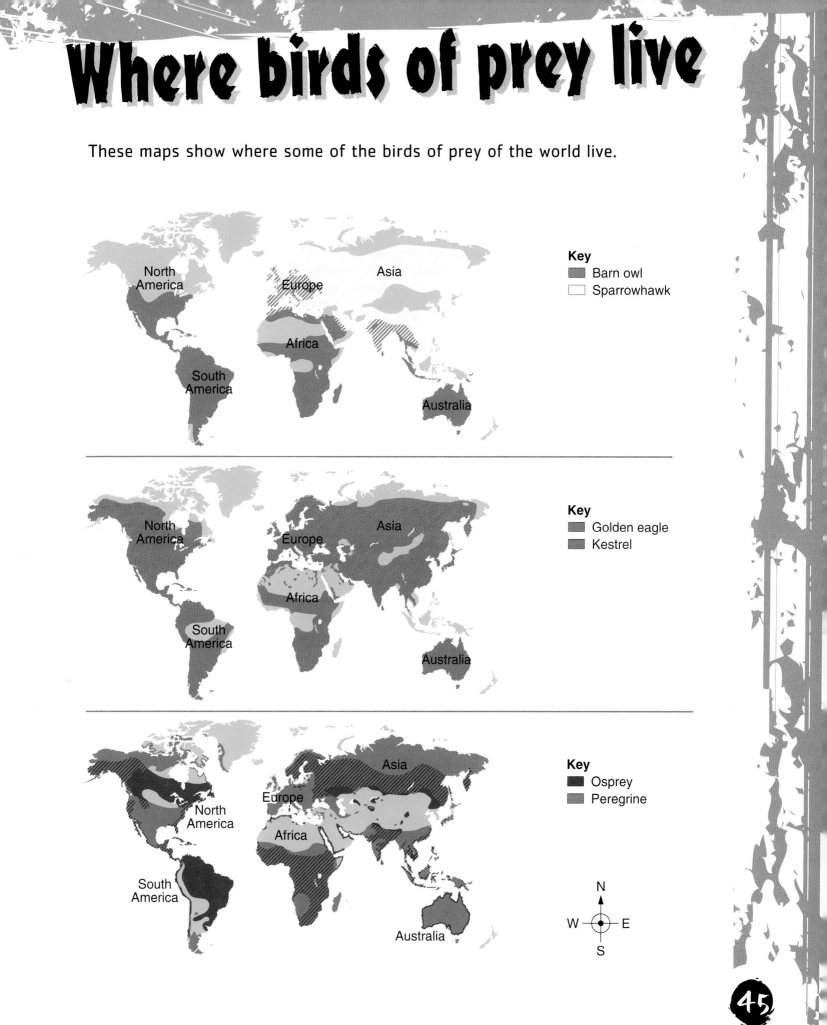

Key
- Barn owl
- Sparrowhawk

Key
- Golden eagle
- Kestrel

Key
- Osprey
- Peregrine

Glossary

acids chemicals that are sharp-tasting or can burn

adapted having special features that help a living thing survive in a particular place

breed mate and produce young

breeding ground area where a group of birds breed each year

breeding season time of year when a group of birds mates and has young

camouflage colouring and markings on a bird or other animal that help it blend in with its background

carrion dead and often rotting meat

cold-blooded animal whose body temperature changes with the temperature of its environment

communal made or used by a group of animals or people

conifer evergreen tree such as fir or pine

conservationists people who try to prevent the loss of wildlife and wild habitats

courtship trying to win a partner to mate with

diurnal active in the daytime

endangered when an animal or plant species is in danger of being wiped out completely

falconer someone who keeps birds of prey and trains them to hunt when the falconer asks them to

family group or genera of living things that are closely related

fledge/fledging when a young bird has all the feathers it needs to be able to fly

habitat place where a bird or other creature lives

hide place where a bird-watcher can watch birds without being seen by them

home range for birds of prey, the area around the bird's nesting site where it hunts for food

immune not affected by something

incubate to keep eggs warm so that they will hatch

mammal hairy or furry warm-blooded animal that feeds its young on breast milk

mate/mating when a male inserts sperm into a female animal to fertilize her eggs

migrate to travel long distances every year from summer breeding grounds to winter feeding grounds

moult when a bird moults it gradually loses its old feathers and new ones replace them

pesticide chemical used by farmers to get rid of insect pests

plumage bird's feathers

predator animal that hunts other animals (its prey) for food

prey any animal that is hunted by a predator

raptor bird of prey

rodents animals such as rats, mice, chipmunks and squirrels

roost/roosting place where a bird regularly settles to rest or sleep

savannah grassland in Africa that is dotted with trees and bushes

scavenger animal that eats scraps, dead meat or anything that it can find

spawn when fish spawn, the females release their eggs into the water and the males fertilize them

species group of animals or plants that are all very similar and can breed together to produce fertile young

talons strong feet with hooked claws

temperate region where the climate is neither particularly hot nor particularly cold

territory for birds of prey, an area around a bird's nest, usually smaller than the home range, that birds defend against other birds of the same species

thermal patch of warm, rising air

tundra cold, bleak lands in the Arctic or on high mountains that are covered with snow for large parts of the year

ultraviolet high-energy light that humans cannot see

Further information

Books

Birds of Prey (Nature Factfile), Robin Kerrod and Kim Taylor (Photographer) (Southwater Books, 2002). An illustrated guide to birds of prey with specially commissioned photographs.

Birds of Prey, Ian Newton (consulting editor) (Weldon Owen, 1990). A detailed and comprehensive book covering birds of prey around the world.

Owls of the World: Their Lives, Behavior and Survival, James R. Duncan (Firefly Books, 2003). A book that covers all aspects of owls, including threats to the survival of some species.

Birds of Prey (Peterson Field Guides for Young Naturalists), Jonathan P Latimer, Karen Stray Nolting and Roger Tory Peterson (illustrator) (Houghton Mifflin, 2000). This field guide covers the birds of prey you are likely to see in Britain and Europe.

Birds of Prey: An Introduction to Familiar North American Species (Pocket Naturalist), James Kavanagh and Raymond Leung (illustrator) (Waterford Press, 2002). A field guide for identifying North American birds of prey.

Classifiying Living Things: Birds, Andrew Solway (Heinemann Library, 2003). This books covers the classification of all birds, including falcons and owls.

Websites

www.rspb.org.uk
Europe's largest bird and wildlife conservation charity. The RSPB, The Lodge, Sandy, Bedfordshire, UK, SG19 2DL

www.audubon.org
The most important bird conservation charity in America. National Audubon Society, 700 Broadway, New York, NY 10003, USA

www.hawk-conservancy.org/birdmenu.shtml
Excellent information about birds of prey around the world.

www.owlpages.com/
A packed website with anything you will ever want to know about owls.

www.buteo.com/
An excellent site for American birds of prey.

Index

Titles in the *Wild Predators!* series include:

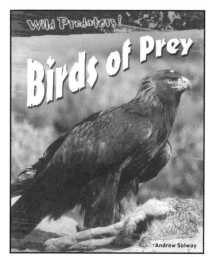

Hardback   0 431 18992 7

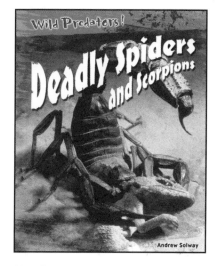

Hardback   0 431 18994 3

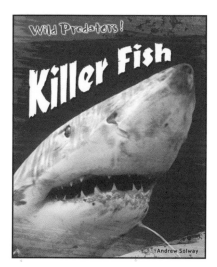

Hardback   0 431 18991 9

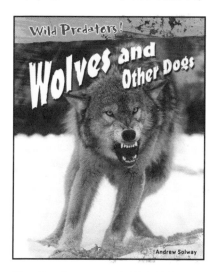

Hardback   0 431 18995 1

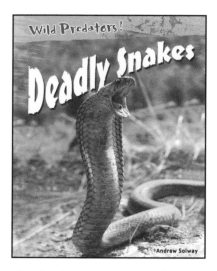

Hardback   0 431 18993 5

Find out about the other Heinemann Library titles on our website www.heinemann.co.uk/library